D0226751

HAUS CURIOSITIES

The Power of Journalists

About the Contributors

Claire Foster-Gilbert is the founder director of the Westminster Abbey Institute. A current and former member of numerous ethics committees, Foster-Gilbert has played an instrumental role in the medical research ethics field, and has led efforts to shift the Church's thinking on environmental issues.

Nick Robinson is the presenter of BBC Radio 4's *Today* programme.

Gary Gibbon is the political editor of Channel 4 News.

Barbara Speed is the opinion editor of the *i* newspaper.

Charlie Beckett is the director of the Polis think-tank at the London School of Economics (LSE).

Edited and with an Introduction by Claire Foster-Gilbert

THE POWER OF JOURNALISTS

Nick Robinson, Gary Gibbon,
Barbara Speed and Charlie Beckett

First published by Haus Publishing in 2018
4 Cinnamon Row
London SW11 3TW
www.hauspublishing.com

A CIP catalogue record for this book is
available from the British Library

Print ISBN: 978-1-912208-25-8
Ebook ISBN: 978-1-912208-26-5

Typeset in Garamond by MacGuru Ltd

Printed in Spain

Contents

Acknowledgements

Sincere thanks are due to the Dean and Chapter of Westminster, the Council of Reference and Steering Group of Westminster Abbey Institute, Ruth Cairns, Frances D'Souza, Mark Easton, Harry Hall, Peter Hennessy, Kathleen James, Ann Leslie, Brian Leveson, Seán Moore, David Neuberger, Sally Osman, Barbara Schwepcke, Jean Seaton, Jo Stimpson, Sunbeam House in Hastings and Moore's Cottage, Knockanure, County Kerry.

Introduction

Claire Foster-Gilbert

In 2016, Westminster Abbey Institute held a series of dialogues on the role and power of the media in public life. This book comprises essays based upon the words of four of the contributors, which were at least partly informed by the other contributors, Ann Leslie and Jean Seaton. This introduction offers some context for the series, held within the ancient walls of Westminster Abbey on Parliament Square; an account of the different sorts of media we enjoy today; a reflection on their public service role in the ecology of a healthy constitutional democracy; and an introduction to the essayists.

Westminster Abbey Institute was founded to nurture and revitalise moral and spiritual values in public life and service, and to promote the value of public service more generally. It works with those traditionally regarded as public servants – such as politicians, civil servants, judges, teachers, healthcare practitioners and members of the Armed Forces and Police – and also with journalists. There is a common view, not only among those in public life, that the media are not part of the company of those seeking to serve the common good; rather, they are its enemy. This is a view the Institute has consistently and strenuously resisted. The value of a free press cannot be overstated: it is an essential characteristic of a civilised society. By means of our free press, the activities of Government, business and foreign powers can be called to account, without fear of reprisal. We may loathe the crude headlines and bemoan their lack of accuracy, but suppose our press were prevented by our Government from creating them? Imagine reading a news story that we knew had been censored or even generated by the Government: how soon would we start to mistrust the Government? Ann Leslie, who has reported from numerous countries which do not enjoy the privilege of a free press, quoted Tom Stoppard approvingly:[1] 'No matter how imperfect things are, if you've got a free press everything is correctable, and without it everything is concealable.'[2] The irony is that our trust, such as it is, arises precisely because the Government allows itself to be criticised, often unfairly, in the press. And yet our assumption can be that we mistrust the Government *because* of the media's reporting. We probably take the invisible underlying trust for granted. We would miss it sorely were its protections to be too much corroded in what Marilynne Robinson has memorably called 'the acid bath of cynicism'.[3]

The UK media consist of, first, broadcast media – television, radio and internet – some of which are governed by statute and funded non-commercially. Second are the written media – print newspapers and journals and their online counterparts, as well as digital-only news websites. None of this second group is governed by specific statutes, although, to state the obvious, all are bound by the laws of the land (and, as they turn increasingly to video footage, they begin to resemble broadcasters, raising a question about whether they should fall under Ofcom regulation) and all of them have to find their own funding, either commercially or through donations. People are, third, increasingly also receiving their news through online platforms that are not themselves news organisations, such as Google and Facebook. The definition of 'news' is itself becoming frayed, as it is taken to encompass the full mixture of information, assertion, argument, emotion, comment and cultural influence through which people inform themselves.

The BBC – where Nick Robinson, one of the essayists in this volume, works – and Channel 4 – where another contributor, Gary Gibbon, works – are both governed by statute which requires them to be public service broadcasters first and foremost. The Royal Charter governing the BBC requires it to 'inform, educate and entertain' all licence-fee payers. The trust the BBC has earned over the decades since it was founded remains measurably significant: 92% of UK adults in online homes use BBC television, radio or online media each week,[4] and during the Brexit referendum campaign, the BBC was the most used source of information for voters.[5] For the BBC, the public service requirement was supported from its establishment in 1927 by a funding model that protected it from commercial and political pressures. The BBC licence fee, set by Government (currently at £150.50 per year) and payable by anyone who has a television or uses BBC iPlayer, means the BBC has a revenue of £3.5 billion a year to spend independently. The funding model ensures political and commercial independence, and it also lays a requirement on the BBC to serve all of the UK universally. But since both the principle of the licence fee and its size have to be renegotiated regularly with different Governments, the director-general and chair of the BBC cannot ignore politics. Moreover, the Government of the day may seek to change the rule book. For example, in July 2015 the Government decided that it would no longer pay the licence fees of over-75s. This had been seen as a welfare provision, and it was cut. After a heated battle, the BBC agreed to take the cost upon itself, rather than impose a charge which could arguably have significant health implications; this means the BBC's income will be reduced by £800 million as the change is implemented. Despite battles such as these, which require negotiating skills and a keen political sense, the model is one which, for the most part, allows the BBC the independence to navigate between the Scylla of commercial pressures debasing quality and universality and the Charybdis of political pressures undermining impartiality.

Channel 4 was created by the Broadcasting Act 1980 and came on air for the first time in November 1982. It is commercially funded but publicly owned, which means that it shares a similar duty of public service to that of the BBC, but without the funding model to protect it against commercial pressures. Nevertheless, its commitment to impartiality, expressed by Channel 4's political editor Gary Gibbon in his essay, is palpable. He sees it as a value utterly essential for a democratically engaged society.

The newspaper world in which Barbara Speed, a third contributor to this volume, works is not governed by the same legal requirement to be impartial, and the tradition of editorial favouring of different political parties or individuals is a long one. Attempts to regulate the press in the face of sometimes shockingly bad behaviour are fraught with controversy, as the recent Leveson enquiry and subsequent report found.[6] Attempts to enact its recommendation for a new press regulator have met resistance: IMPRESS is the only regulator to have signed up to all the Leveson principles, but few newspapers or other media outlets have joined IMPRESS, arguing that to do so would be to undermine their independence. Some accept the self-regulating regimes of the Independent Press Standards Organisation (IPSO) and the Editor's Code. The internet is even more of a 'Wild West' of unregulated territory, thanks to the near-instant uploading of moment-by-moment reporting and commenting. The implications and potential of this still relatively new medium are discussed by both Barbara Speed and fourth contributor Charlie Beckett, formerly a journalist and now an academic. People who were once just passive audiences consuming the news curated by others are now exercising their creative muscles and responding – but the conversation is not, and perhaps never can be, between equals. Emotion is increasing, which softens and colours hard-edged facts and affects the ways in which information is received, digested and answered.

Journalists working within the UK's independent media enjoy the liberty of being able to say what they wish without fear or favour, but this liberty brings with it the responsibility to tell the truth without fear or favour. Telling the truth is a moral responsibility, though Nick Robinson strenuously resists the word 'moral' in his essay. His valid argument is that journalists must not worry about the moral consequences of their reporting. To do so would be to deny what they exist to do, which is to tell the public what is happening, to 'publish and be damned'. But this argument only serves to emphasise the duty to tell the truth, and what could be closer to a moral principle than truth-telling? Journalists are, by this account, non-utilitarian duty-based actors on the public stage. For them, the ends will never justify the means, because they are not interested in ends. Truth-telling, whatever the outcome, is the guiding principle. 'Fake news', then, is a logical impossibility. But, as Charlie Beckett recognises, there is a good end, or consequence, of truth-telling, which is that the public can rely on what they are told and thus become informed participants in our democracy. Charlie pushes the moral point further:

journalists, he argues, should seek to promote 'the good life' by means of the 'good information' they generate. Gary Gibbon agrees: impartial and truthful reporting of well-chosen stories helps, in particular, those who have neither access to the plethora of 'news' sources nor the skills to navigate and make sense of them. Journalists have this responsibility. As Barbara Speed suggests, the very availability of every kind of source to all those with access to the internet can mean that no one questions veracity. Lies spread unchecked. A study published in *Science* demonstrated that, on the internet, untruths are up to 100 times more likely to be passed on, and much more quickly, than truths.[7] We are not good at telling each other the truth online. Journalists are not, then, just speakers of truth, but also guardians of truth; not only do they curate the flood of available information, foregrounding the truth in it, but they also call out lies. Too often 'news' is presented as emotional argument conducted through megaphones, all transmission and no reception. Where an argument is dismissed as a lie or a person as corrupt, Nick Robinson urges, the journalist should raise the question, on what grounds are you making such an accusation? Just because you are on the other side? Truth remains the moral lodestar by which journalists should navigate their professional roles. Fearlessly telling the truth to society is a very great public service.

The journalist's commitment to truth as a guiding principle passes the Gladstonian test of the public servant who must keep private interest out of the public square,[8] but the principle is only as good as the institutions and people who are meant to uphold it. Even for those to whom the public service of journalism is sacrosanct, and even for those who work within media organisations that are required by law to be impartial and have funding models to protect their independence, truth-telling is a challenge. No individual is without their prejudices and partialities, nor can they be sure they have access to accurate and unbiased information. In an essay that is kinder to US journalism than the authors in this book, Helen Boaden observes the 'polite blank stare' and 'raised eyebrow' of a US audience of journalists in response to her enthusiasm for the BBC's core value of impartiality: 'The objective journalist... is viewed with skepticism. Why on earth should journalists have unique powers of objectivity?'[9] Jean Seaton contrasts the US approach that sees the truth emerging out of competition, as the strongest view, with the UK approach, which sees the attempt at impartial truth-telling as more of a honing process:

> [It is] a dynamic and frankly lovely [approach] developed by people who learn and listen to each other, and quite often encounter and listen to people they don't agree with... [L]istening to people that you don't agree with nuances your argument and makes your argument stronger. You have to be able to encounter the strongest argument against

it. That's basically the John Stuart Mill tradition and, in fact, that is one which has infused our institutions.[10]

Nick Robinson writes of the discipline of seeking to come as close to the truth as possible today, always knowing that tomorrow the facts may reveal themselves differently, or more clearly, changing what had been claimed the day before. Charlie Beckett argues that social media has brought about a change in ethos that creates emotional mood music rather than cold facts, and he makes the case for journalists needing to respond to that, reporting with sympathy the 'moral choices, values and feelings' that populate our political discourse, for example, and being honest about one's own partiality as a journalist. For Charlie, the advent of social media has presented journalists with an exciting new opportunity, not to resile from telling the truth, but to explore more deeply and empathetically how that might be done. No one argues that we should abandon the attempt.

The essays in this book demonstrate that the will to come as close as possible to the truth remains at the heart of the bona fide journalist. We the public should feel reassured that this ideal has such tenacity, even as it comes under pressure from all sides. We may be rubbish at telling each other the truth online; our lies may flow much more easily than truths; lying may be our default means of communication; we may only ever express partiality because humans always only ever have partial perceptions; but we do, usually, recognise the truth when we are offered it, or know – and hate it – when we are not. Although we never see it in full, truth still acts as a navigation point, as we somehow know how close to or far away from it we are. It is in our journalists' power to navigate well, and we want them to.

The Essayists

Nick Robinson is a presenter on the BBC's flagship programme *Today*. He writes an award-winning blog, presents a range of BBC television and radio documentaries and discussion programmes and is the author of *Live From Downing Street*[11] and *Election Notebook*.[12] Nick started out in broadcasting at Piccadilly Radio, and worked his way up as a producer on a variety of shows including *Newsround* and *Crimewatch*. He became an assistant producer for *On the Record*, and in 1993 was promoted to deputy editor of *Panorama*. He then switched from working behind the cameras to working in front of them, presenting *Weekend Breakfast* and *Late Night Live* on Radio 5 Live. He later became chief political correspondent on the BBC News channel. He left the BBC in 2002 to become political editor for ITV News, returning to the BBC in 2005 as its political editor until he moved to the *Today* programme in 2015. He has won a string of awards including the Royal Television Society (RTS) Specialist Journalist of the Year, *The House* magazine's Commentator of the

Year, the Political Studies Association Political Journalist of the Year and Editorial Intelligence's Blogger of the Year. Nick's essay is based upon his contribution to a conversation with Ann Leslie, chaired by Frances D'Souza.

Gary Gibbon is political editor of Channel 4 News, a post he has held since 2005. Prior to that he was the programme's political correspondent. He has reported extensively on UK politics, covering six general election campaigns. His 2001 interview with Peter Mandelson triggered the Northern Ireland Secretary's resignation from the Cabinet. In 2005 he broadcast the first account of the Attorney General's legal opinion on the war in Iraq. With Jon Snow, he was jointly awarded the RTS Home News award for that story. In 2008, he was awarded Political Broadcaster of the Year by the Political Studies Association. In 2010, he was awarded RTS Specialist Broadcaster of the Year, and was nominated for the award again in 2015. He is the author of *Breaking Point*.[13] Gary's essay is based upon his contribution to a conversation with Jean Seaton, chaired by David Neuberger.

Barbara Speed is comment editor for the *i* newspaper. She began her career at the *New Statesman* on its urbanism mini-site, *CityMetric*. She helped launch the site, which covers urban policy and living from housing to devolution and maps and has now grown to a very healthy readership (including a sizeable number of map obsessives). She then became the *New Statesman* technology and digital culture writer, and covered stories including Facebook's role in the 2016 American election, concerns around the UK's Investigatory Powers Bill and the rise of YouTuber publishing. She was shortlisted for a Words by Women award for Technology Writer of the Year. She also occasionally covered politics, and published an interview with Jeremy Corbyn in 2015 which confidently predicted he would not make it onto the leadership ballot first time round. Barbara joined the *i* newspaper in 2016, at a time when it has seen a record increase in readers. *Press Gazette* deemed it the only publication to offer truly neutral coverage in the run-up to the EU referendum. Barbara also writes for the *Guardian*, *The Times*, *Times Higher Education*, *The Spectator*, *Private Eye*, the *Evening Standard* and *Vice*. Barbara is a fellow of Westminster Abbey Institute. Her essay is based upon her contribution to a conversation with Charlie Beckett, chaired by Mark Easton.

Charlie Beckett is a professor in the Department of Media and Communications at the London School of Economics (LSE). He is the founding director of Polis, the LSE international journalism institute. He was an award-winning filmmaker and editor at LWT, BBC and ITN. He began his journalism career at the *South London Press* and ended it as a programme editor at Channel 4 News, covering stories such as the terrorist attacks on New York in 2001 and London in 2005. He was a specialist in politics and international affairs. He is the author of *SuperMedia*, which sets out how journalism is being transformed by technological and other changes and how that will impact on society.[14] His second book, *WikiLeaks*, describes the history and significance of WikiLeaks and the wider context of new kinds of disruptive online journalism.[15] Most recently, his research has examined the role of emotion in journalism, how the news media report on terrorism and new forms of engagement through social media. Charlie's institute, Polis, is a public forum for debate about the news media in the UK and globally. It holds seminars, conferences and lectures and has published reports on topics such as social media, political reporting, financial journalism, humanitarian communication and media and development. Charlie's essay is based upon his contribution to a conversation with Barbara Speed, chaired by Mark Easton.

Press Freedom; Press Responsibility

Nick Robinson

Should journalism pass a test that it contributes to the public good? In order to be provocative, I am tempted to say, 'Absolutely not. It is not the job of journalists to think of the consequences of their stories.' I know that stating it so boldly will upset and challenge people. I hope it will provoke a debate.

It is the job of a journalist to ask a few questions, such as 'Is it news? Is it true? Is it fair? Is the context being properly explained?' But we absolutely should not ask, 'What will happen tomorrow if we report this story?' If we did, it would put journalists in an impossible position. In the case of, say, a story about economics, are we to turn ourselves into market traders calculating whether a particular piece of news will lead to a run on the pound, or an economist assessing whether a run on the pound is or isn't a good thing for this or that group in society? I witnessed Robert Peston being badgered again and again with claims that he had somehow talked Britain down when he reported stories such as that Northern Rock was in crisis or that there was a run on the banks. But his job was not to talk Britain up or down economically. His job was to find out what was going on and to report it in a way that was accurate and fair.

I came across this challenge very early in my own career, not with a story I filed initially, but with one on which I did some follow-up reporting: the revelation that there were secret talks happening to bring about peace in Northern Ireland. It's best to look at hard cases when making a point like mine, and this was a hard case. People could say, and they did say, that people's lives were at stake. The revelation of these talks could have sabotaged any capacity to find a way through to what was later called a peace process and the Good Friday Agreement. As a young journalist, I had to decide whether I accepted that analysis, or whether I believed that, in the end, it was more important for reporters to tell society what is going on, and for society then to come to terms with it. I found I did believe it was more important that I should report on the story, even though I also believed that preserving the secrecy of the talks would enable them to continue happening. My reasoning was that if I were to hold back now, I would be embarking on a fool's errand for the rest of my career as a journalist. Such reticence would lead to my questioning every story in this way: if it applied to the Northern Ireland talks, then I should make the same assessment of every story on which I reported. And that would mean that I would be doing the wrong job.

I have personal historical reasons for feeling so strongly about this, supported by my research into the history of journalism about politics. My grandparents were German-Jewish, refugees from the Nazis who were lucky to get out in time. They had been forced out by the Nazis and chose to flee to Shanghai, where they soon had to flee again, this time from the communists. They ended up in Switzerland; they were lucky to have escaped the Holocaust, unlike many families. As a very young boy I would sit with my grandfather as he turned the big round dials on one of those enormous Roberts radios. He would turn the dials, going through the foreign networks, and I could hear the voices of Russians and then the French, and then the voices of Americans and finally the BBC, which is where he stayed. This was because it was a network he'd learned that he could trust. The reason my grandfather was so obsessed with listening to his radio news bulletin in total silence each and every day was that he had come to trust the BBC as an arbiter of the truth – or, rather, as close as you could possibly get to the truth. He started his listening in Shanghai, ignoring the ban on radios there at the time. Imprisonment was threatened if you had a radio, but he and my mother and her mother would hide in a cupboard every day to listen to the BBC news. That is the personal reason I believe in the power of journalism to do good overall if it concentrates on truthful reporting.

My interest in the history of political journalism grew as I researched my book *Live From Downing Street*.[16] I was struck by how it was that, again and again, people in positions of power and authority thought that if only they could determine what was responsible journalism, things would be better. For many years, at least between the 16th and the 18th centuries, that meant a total ban on reporting what MPs said. That is extraordinary to consider. I remember the much more recent arguments about whether or not the House of Commons debates should be televised, which was evidence of the same concern to try and control what information reached the public. But this ban was total. It was only overturned after a great battle in 1771 between the Prime Minister, Lord North, who is rather more famous for losing America, and John Wilkes. There was an actual battle, a riot in which Lord North's carriage was attacked and his hat was knocked off his head. Apparently this upset him more than anything else, because it was his favourite hat. The battle to reassert the right of journalists to report what was said in the House of Commons was won, though the ridiculous law was retained until the early 19th century.

I am, then, deeply suspicious of people who want to define what reporters should and shouldn't do. My premise is that you should report as much as possible. However, I recognise this hard line throws up dilemmas. Take, for example, the reporting of MPs' expenses. There is no doubt that the story in 2009 did great damage to the standing of our democratic institutions, and that I regret. The reporting gave many people the impression that all elected officials were on the take. I not only regret that impression, I think it is untrue, and I have over time tried to use whatever position I have to demonstrate that it is not true. However, that does not mean that I think it would have been right to suppress the information. I don't; indeed, it had to be dragged out of the authorities. It was a Freedom of Information request that first produced the information that led to questions about expenses and the so-called John Lewis List. That eventually led to the data being assembled on a disk that was then sold illegally to *The Daily Telegraph*, which took the risk of printing it. My own organisation wasn't offered the disk, but would have been very unlikely to have taken that risk. *The Times* turned down the opportunity. So, are we better as a society because that information is out? I think that, for all the wrongs that it incurred, we probably are, because a system that was corrupt, with the people it involved knowing it was corrupt, eventually had to be exposed.

There are issues occasionally about privacy that have to be dealt with, though less often for me than for those who work in tabloid journalism. Again, I'm generally inclined to argue that you have to follow the policy, the old slogan, of 'publish and be damned'. Where people have told me that their personal lives have no bearing on their public office, invariably I have discovered that they have. David Blunkett, a man I like and admire, ended up having to resign because he had obtained a visa for his lover's nanny. We only knew he'd obtained a visa for his lover's nanny because somebody had written about his lover. It was difficult and painful. I conducted his first interview after he resigned, and we shed a tear together, but do I think it was the right thing to do? I'm afraid I do.

Then there is the dilemma of entrapment in order to hold people to account. Sam Allardyce was secretly filmed by *The Daily Telegraph*, allegedly offering advice on how to get round The Football Association's rules on player transfers and negotiating a £400,000 deal for himself. In the world of politics, *Dispatches* used secret cameras to expose what it claimed was an abuse of parliamentary rules by Sir Malcolm Rifkind and Jack Straw. Both men said the accusation was untrue at the time, and they were both cleared of any wrongdoing. But here's my challenge: for every one of those stings which you may have found distasteful or felt was disproportionate, there was another which revealed important, shocking truths, such as *Panorama* exposing the care home scandal which led to care homes being closed and standards in others being improved. It was only by entrapment or secret filming that we were able to get close to the truth.

I am not proposing anarchy. There are rules. The BBC has its own rules in addition to being regulated by Ofcom. The BBC's code of practice for secret filming, for example, means it cannot just be done on a whim. If we want to do it, we have to demonstrate through an internal process that there is evidence of wrongdoing and that it can only be proved by pursuing it using covert recording. There's no doubt that Donald

Trump's privacy was breached when a tape of his private conversation on a bus was broadcast, revealing his sexist attitudes and behaviour. Would we rather he had a say on whether his privacy were breached? Or would we rather journalists 'publish and be damned'?

Being damned is not the same as being irresponsible, and journalists as a community are not wholly irresponsible. I'm going to tell the following story in code, for reasons which I hope will become obvious. There was a crisis in Tony Blair's family while he was in Downing Street – what looked like an emergency in the family. Nobody reported it. If you search for it now, you will find that no mainstream news outlet mentions it, not the *Daily Mail*, nor the BBC – no one. There are some blogs which argue that there was a 'wicked conspiracy' to hide the truth. But the actual truth is that there was a personal crisis within the family, and it was over relatively quickly. We all knew about it. It's fair to say that everyone assumed that one or other paper or broadcaster would break the news first, and we were nervous about being left out of covering the story. As it happens, the paper that wanted to break the news was the *Observer*. But in order to look less bad, the editor of the *Observer* rang the editor of *The Mail on Sunday* and said, 'If you break the news, we will too. That way we can share the flack.' To the credit of the editor of *The Mail on Sunday*, he told the *Observer* editor, 'If you want to breach somebody's privacy like that, you should go ahead and do it, but we will all condemn you.' I heard this story from my own editor at ITV news, where I was working at the time. I had thought that ITV might have adopted a more ethically fluid attitude and been bolder, but in fact no one reported the story, and to this day that is the case.

I don't claim to produce The Truth, and we should be suspicious of anybody who does. I am only too aware that the truth I discover today may tomorrow turn out to be not quite so true after all, or just a glimpse of the truth. Nevertheless, my experience of journalists, not just at the BBC but also at ITV, and the many others I have come across in my working life, is that the vast majority of us are motivated by trying to get as close to the truth as we can that day, and that motivation is what guides our work each day. That doesn't mean we are not capable of getting things horribly wrong, and it also doesn't mean that our backgrounds – where we're brought up; our religious backgrounds; our prejudices; our tendency to be liberal, metropolitan types – don't distort our ideas of what the truth looks like. But the task remains to get as close as possible to the truth, as best we can.

The question is: what sort of truth should we be aiming for? Especially in a so-called post-truth society, I would champion factual truth. There is a real and growing need for journalism to tell us what the factual bases for debates are. The classic misleading piece of campaign literature in our recent history is the Brexit Leave campaign bus with its claim, 'We send the

EU £350 million a week; let's fund our NHS instead.' I know how this calculation was reached – take the £19 billion annual contribution to the EU and divide it by 52. However, that £19 billion is a gross figure and doesn't take into account all that the UK receives back in subsidies. But for me, the crucial word to call out is 'send'. If that word had not been used, the truth of the claim would have been easier to defend, even though it gave many people the false impression that if we left the EU we would give the NHS £350 million a week. The slogan did not actually say that. But 'send' is simply untrue, and I said so on air, because at no time did anyone send that amount or ask for that amount to be sent. I do think we need journalism which is bolder in the way it deals with preposterous claims that undermine factual truth.

The same is not the case for what we might call moral truth. Journalists shouldn't adhere to one group's definition of morality at the expense of another section of the public that defines morality differently. We cannot take the role of arbiters of moral truth, and that is why the BBC has a requirement to be impartial. However, that is not to say that we are morally disabled. I am not expected to be impartial about racism, for example. I am not obliged to say that some people think some races are inferior and others do not, and leave it at that. Perhaps there are also other areas about which we should not be impartial, but I am nervous about creating too many of them.

Of course, impartiality is hard enough to sustain at the best of times. We all have inherent biases, and newspapers have these explicitly. The BBC is required by law to be impartial, so it has to aim for that. It is helped enormously by the way it is organised, neither as a state funded broadcaster nor as a commercial one. But it is not perfect. Rather like democracy, of which it has been said that it is the worst possible political system apart from all the others, the BBC model is the worst for broadcasting apart from all the others we've seen on the planet. The BBC requires legislation and requires Government approval for the size of its budget; hence there is no doubt that the BBC can from time to time become liable to political pressure. It's an illusion to pretend that it isn't. But it's all the more important, then, that as many safeguards as possible are built in to mitigate and limit it. Setting the licence fee in advance for as long as possible is essential, in my view, because if it were set in the shorter term, this or that Chancellor or Prime Minister could haggle over the size of the licence fee for political gain. Once the BBC is treated as if it were a Government department begging for funds, it becomes part of the taxation system. We would find ourselves each year asking if we should trade *Strictly Come Dancing* for a hospital. The licence fee, set in advance and held steady for a lengthy period, creates an arm's-length relationship with Government. Anything that compromises that independence is dangerous. And the way the BBC is run is a lot better than the current alternatives, as I have said. The model which is common in continental Europe allows any new president to sack the state broadcaster: a new head of government means a new head of the state channel. In the United States, there is no public service broadcasting, and there are now no shared facts as the foundation for political debates: political activists on the Right watch Fox News and political activists on the Left watch MSNBC. There was no agreement on facts about healthcare at the end of Obama's administration. People either believed, with Fox News, that Obama was planning socialist death camps, or believed, with MSNBC, that Republicans were in favour of killing the poor. So for all the warts and flaws of broadcasting in the UK, and there are plenty, at least you have people who every day come to work and do their best to get about as close to the truth as they can that day – and that seems to be better than most of the alternatives.

Such an attitude is all the more important because we live in a more intolerant climate than ever – one which, I would argue, is reflected in the press rather than created by the press. I had my own experience of this when I was reporting on the Scottish independence referendum. I became a hate figure for some of the most ardent campaigners for independence. Four thousand people marched on the BBC's Glasgow headquarters behind a banner saying 'Nick "the Liar" Robinson'. The banner was about 30 feet wide. It was an intimidating experience – not particularly for me, because I had become thick skinned, and I think I'm paid to put up with such attacks – but certainly for some of my younger colleagues, who'd had no experience of such behaviour before. Such behaviour comes out of a climate in which to attack the motives of people you disagree with has become fashionable. We could be reporting on the rise of nationalism in Scotland, or the rise of the UK Independence Party (UKIP), or the rise of the Corbynistas. Each of these groups, and others like them who feel they're not the establishment and feel threatened by the 'men in suits', are expressing their anger more vociferously, and the rage seems to be increasing. It seems to me that newspapers, and to a certain extent politicians as well, feel that they have to follow this rage. This shows itself in inflated language and arguments, as if everyone must raise their voices to get anybody to notice anything at all. Inasmuch as an organisation like the BBC has a responsibility, it is to hose down the rage somewhat, and to challenge preposterous claims made during campaigns about the motives of opposing sides, such as that they are lying or that they are corrupt. I think we could do more to call out such claims, asking, blandly, 'What do you mean by "they're corrupt"? Do you mean you disagree with them?'

In the end, I am at my most contented as a journalist when I feel I have made the world easier to understand. Not when a viewer says, 'Here, aren't you that bloke off the telly and weren't you rude to George Bush once?' Rather, when they say, 'You helped me understand that; I found it complicated and you helped me understand.' The world is a fantastically complicated place, and a rather frightening one. In the face of people who would have me shot or beaten up, I've never shown the personal bravery or the determination that some investigative reporters have, but there's a role for men in suits like me, which is to try our best to help people to understand better the choices they – we as a society – have to make.

Press Impartiality

Gary Gibbon

As a lobby correspondent, I'm not exactly on the front line of hazardous reporting. But on 13th April, 2002 I descended the steps into the paper-strewn fire hazard of Tony Benn's basement flat in London's Notting Hill. Surrounded by shelves and piles of archive newspaper cuttings and diaries, Benn did what he always did on these occasions, and set down his own tape recorder to be sure he had his own record of what he'd said, in case of misrepresentation, to make sure he could hold me to account.

On this occasion, he raised a fresh gripe with the mainstream media. 'Why is it that I have to look at you, Gary, when you're interviewing me, but when you address the people, you get to stare straight into the lens?' he said. 'You're putting yourself up as God – the ultimate judge.' And, in some ways, he was right.

Journalists are held to account by regulators – in the case of broadcasters in the UK, by Ofcom or the BBC. But on a daily basis, we try to judge the line of impartiality that we are required to follow, which is set out clearly in Ofcom's Broadcasting Code and the BBC's Editorial Guidelines. To Benn, it looked a bit like we, as a breed, were claiming that what we said was the truth. I can see why he feared that, and his political descendants in the current Labour leadership strongly echo his views in their disparagement of mainstream media. We should be held to account, and we are anything but gods. But the current political climate means that impartial broadcasting – the attempt to stare down the lens and give people your best stab at an unbiased, objective take on events – is not just a worthwhile endeavour but as important as it has ever been.

As Lord Neuberger pointed out in the 2016 Westminster Abbey Institute dialogue from which this essay is drawn, standards of impartiality in broadcasting, required in the UK by law, have always come under pressure, as broadcasters have had to worry about viewing figures and to tread an uneasy line between impartiality and popularity. It's a line the newspapers and the 'Wild West' of the internet do not have to be concerned with, as no legal requirement to be impartial has been placed upon them. And it's a line the US walked away from in 1987, when its rules on impartial news broadcasting were dropped under President Reagan.

The responsibilities of fair and balanced reporting start before the reporter has opened their mouth. One of the biggest entrusted powers is the 'running order' of the bulletin. What is judged to be the most important story, and how much time do you permit it? In an idealised bulletin, you might lead with what history would judge to be important when it looks back at that day. But the pressures of audience fatigue, novelty and competition are rivals to those higher goals.

In the business of reporting itself, we've long been used to challenges from the political parties to stop being so 'establishment' (from the Left) and stop being so 'lefty' (from the Right). The attacks are sometimes meant to make you a bit more lenient on the side mounting the onslaught when you next cover them. They are sometimes less brazenly cynical and reflect a passionate feeling that the broadcaster is simply missing the bigger picture, and is trapped in a bubble or seeing events through a restrictive prism. Whatever the spur, those pressures are intensifying with the polarisation of our politics.

In the UK, in the aftermath of the EU referendum (and in Scotland, on the back of its referendum on independence), people are finding it harder to see that any virtue or good intent lurks in their opponents' arguments. Issues like independence and Brexit take a special hold on people's emotions as well as their intellects. On top of that, people are struggling with the complexity of rapid moving events and technology that can leave them more puzzled than ever about how to vote or about what powers governments really have.

This is an environment in which broadcasters, with their rules of impartiality, have never been more necessary in my lifetime. Viewers, listeners and voters need and sometimes crave help navigating the arguments and counterarguments, the rhetoric and the facts. The best, albeit imperfect, bet for delivering that is the rule set we work by, and the brassy alternative is on technicolour display across the pond.

In the US, you can see powerful media, driven by commercial forces, using algorithms and sometimes the brittlest of framings in language and coverage to draw viewers or online customers deeper and deeper into the cave of their own prejudices or instincts. The end product – useful to the purveyor but not, I would argue, to a functioning society – is a more entrenched or polarised individual, hardened against the alternative perspective. The channels don't give the audience breadth or context, pure data or balance. They ignite indignation that feeds the need for more of the same. The UK's impartial broadcast reporting ecology is under pressure and needs friends. The audience for fixed-time bulletins has been in decline as other outlets challenge it.[17] This format already competes with companies like Facebook tailoring news bites to fit each person's profile and keep them in their comfort zone. Broadcast news in the UK is still a trusted provider of impartiality, but there are doubts creeping into public perceptions.[18]

The biggest challenge to our impartiality culture in political broadcast reporting came with the referendum on EU membership and continues in its aftermath. The EU referendum campaigns were among the shrillest and most unappetising contests we've ever seen in our democracy – in the words of the man who became Theresa May's first chief of staff, it was full of 'poison'.[19] Imagine, then, what it would have been like if all the people on one side had only received their news from one source that entirely reflected their opinions, and all the people on the other side had a similar service catered to them. We may have been nudged closer to that situation than we have been before. The online efforts of the campaigns to focus their potential voters on highly partial messaging were significant and, some senior figures in the Leave camp think, critical to the outcome.

How well did the broadcast media perform under these special pressures? I think we bent over backwards in an effort to be balanced, and in the process sometimes lost our balance. Under the duty of impartiality, it is not 'job done' when you give both sides an equal hearing and then swiftly move on to the next topic. We know that in science reporting, and we were in danger of forgetting it in our political reporting amidst the special pressures and intensity of 2016. One of our primary duties is to subject differing propositions to the same rigour. If one of those propositions collapses like a meringue under fact-based, evidence driven questioning, that is not a failure of impartiality. Nervous newsrooms, knowingly peopled by the demographic that tended to support Remain (London graduates et al), seemed wary of chasing down some Leave arguments with rigorous analysis. There was an understandable self-policing exercise that, I think – well intentioned though it was – perverted news judgements. One instance that stays in my mind is the publication of a report by the Institute for Fiscal Studies (IFS), painstaking research carried out with scrupulous independence.[20] It suggested the economy would take a hit from Brexit, damaging economic growth and therefore the tax take. The official Leave campaign put forward Iain Duncan Smith with a tackle on the man, not the ball. He attacked the IFS for being 'funded by the EU'. In fact, only 11% of IFS funding comes from the EU. One BBC bulletin I heard actually led with that attack. The programme editor probably thought the top line of the bulletin should ping backwards and forwards between Leave and Remain in pursuit of some notion of balance. But a weighty piece of research from a 'stare down the lens' organisation that aims for objectivity itself didn't deserve that treatment, and, more importantly, the listeners deserved better.

One channel actually operated a stopwatch approach to its coverage, and did so pretty strictly within individual bulletins and reports. Balancing the coverage over a period makes more sense and can allow you to let individuals develop their arguments over more than a sound bite. You might have Gisela Stuart, one of the most compelling and popular advocates of Leave, speaking at length over a long discursive film one night on Channel 4 News followed a few nights later by Hilary Benn, actually speaking to me in St Margaret's Church next door to the Abbey, making the case for Remain.

The challenge to me over the EU referendum campaign was

whether or not we engaged voters enough in the arguments on both sides. In truth, how many people voting in June 2016 understood the European Single Market, the EU Customs Union or the complexities of Free Trade Agreements? The news bulletin must tell you what is new that day, and with two official campaigns that could mean – and was often interpreted as meaning – 'what is it that campaign A or B wants us to report today?' But what campaigns are doing day after day in a contest like this is finding grabby language, aggressive attacks or scary numbers to reinforce exactly what they just said the day before. We broadcasters can be suckers for this. The campaigns know it and play on it. This was never more the case than in the strange world of a referendum campaign where you had wares being sold by the political equivalent of pop-up stores.[21] The Tory-influenced cross-party campaign groups, who were entitled to dominate the coverage under Ofcom rules, were not accountable in the way that a political party running in a general election to become the Government is accountable. Promises and scares become more reckless when they don't have to be accounted for later. The Leave campaign, for instance, was not a 'government-in-waiting', but it issued manifestos as if it were. A news bulletin can't resist an exciting new top line, and the news bulletins reporting that Leave were promising an Australian-style points-based immigration system must have left many voters thinking that was what they were going to get if they voted Leave. It was designed to do just that. Efforts to give the Leave camp a fair crack of the whip (plus the pressure for a fresh and interesting lead story) should not have restrained the duty to scrutinise what was actually being offered: a promise they couldn't deliver, as they were a 'here today, gone tomorrow' temporary campaign coalition, not a government.

I've focused on broadcast journalism because of the legal obligations under which we operate and for which I think we should be eternally grateful. But I should say there are awesome journalists working in the written media who strive for the same standards and whom I look up to for what they achieve in uncovering what's going on with impartiality and integrity. But we all know that the newspapers operate under huge commercial pressures. Even the best journalists in the written media find themselves under pressure to conform to the proprietor's wishes, the editorial slant, the line to take. As populists swipe at 'facts' and 'evidence', there has never been a more important time for us to have impartial reporting, a well from which you know you can drink the water. There are sugary drinks galore in the market place. They will be provided. We need to guard our fresh water well.

The rules on impartial reporting help our democracy function and can help people accept the otherness of others in a way that strident partisan broadcasting does not. They can foster a sense of shared endeavour in a way in which screeching factionalism does not. And it's not just shock jocks and algorithm-driven newsfeeds that can drive us into separate silos. Look at the US and you can see that people aren't just getting their news from completely distinct bias-reinforcing outlets. People are physically more in silos too, choosing residential areas that match their outlook.[22] In Britain, the EU membership referendum threw a light on divisions that had been neglected, and on resentments and silos of our own. But we still have, just about, a table where the nation breaks bread together. Bulletin viewing figures across the networks might be in a gradual decline, but they surge at times of crisis, concern and national moment. There is a residual sense that this is some kind of national hearth.

The recent trend towards fact-checking, pioneered in the UK by Channel 4 News, is one extra tool for impartial reporting, but I think it comes with a health warning. I think there's a tendency in newsrooms to park the fact-checking in an online silo of its own, or to say, 'We fact-checked that on our daytime coverage,' when fact-checking should course through everything we do. You can't hide the rigour somewhere else. No reporter should end a bulletin by saying, 'After this piece, you can go and find out what it meant and whether it was true or not somewhere else'.

In the end, press impartiality matters because democracy depends upon it. It is about giving voters some of the tools with which they can exercise their democratic responsibilities. The mood and tone we deploy is also critical. I'm very struck by the impatience that technological advances breed – and the silos of happy selfishness they can breed too. We can't wait a nanosecond for iPhone information, and we choose our own sound world on the train, flick between channels and tracks, shop and change the temperature in the room with instant effect. Politics is a strange and wonderful thing that, by contrast, involves compromise, and compromise among millions moves at a glacial pace.

We mustn't play God, but we must do our best to keep impartiality alive. And we must be held to account. I will end by telling you what Tony Benn did just after our interview in 2002. He said, 'I tell you what, I'm going to look straight into the camera for a change, Gary, because I am going to record something right now, which is my own obituary.' Happily, it would be quite a few years before we would use the footage. He turned to the camera, stared directly into the lens and said, 'I'd like to thank my family and all the people who helped me through life and all the people who supported me in politics, and I hope I didn't give offence.' Then he paused, looked right into the camera again, wagging his finger, and said, 'And I'll check that on transmission.'

Technology and Journalism

Barbara Speed

Which changed the world more dramatically: the first email ever sent, or the first tweet ever posted? Alberto Ibargüen, president of the Knight Foundation, a non-profit body which invests in journalism in the US, would argue that it was the latter. He said in 2016 that the advent of social media was a disruption to the written word comparable with Johannes Gutenberg's invention of the mechanised printing press in the 15th century.[23]

Gutenberg's invention fundamentally changed the nature of the relationship between those writing and those reading. For four and a half millennia, books were handwritten on bits of clay or stone, and later on paper. They were shared around by hand too, and were often lost or destroyed.

After Gutenberg's press was invented, authors suddenly weren't just writing for the people who could get their hands on their single manuscript, or a couple of handmade copies. Their work could be read by hundreds or even thousands of people all over the world. And 'author' no longer meant only the person with access to scribes, or the commitment to copy out their work themselves and hand it around. As Ibargüen put it, 'After Gutenberg, any Tom, Dick or Martin Luther could print whatever they wanted, and it took a hundred years to figure out, to sort it all out.'[24]

Arguably, this is a bit of an exaggeration: according to an analysis done in 2009, the number of books produced in the first 100 years of the press's existence was a tiny fraction of the number that would be produced between 1700 and 1800.[25] But the shift Ibargüen is describing is mostly conceptual: authorship, in the way we understand it today, was born with the dawn of the mass production of books.

Early iterations of the World Wide Web were really no great leap forward from this, except in terms of scale and the fact that you didn't need paper anymore. Admittedly, before its invention, Tom, Dick or Martin Luther had to get past the gatekeeper of whoever ran the presses (or buy their own) to publish, whereas now anyone with an internet connection and some technical know-how can post a website online. But in terms of reader and audience, things remained remarkably similar, considering the complexity of the technology involved: authors still wrote, and readers still read. It was a one-way trans-action, with those who passively consumed information vastly outnumbering those producing and posting it.

But with the rise of social media (part of the development known as Web 2.0) the nature of audience has utterly changed once again. This time, the extent of the change may mean that the concept of 'audience' disappears altogether.

The word 'audience' calls to mind a silent crowd, facing in one direction, absorbing information from a source. It comes from the Latin word *audentia*, meaning a hearing or a listening. But now the audience is all over the place, facing all sorts of different sources – and, crucially, audience members can talk back. In fact, they can talk back to such an extent that the power of the original piece of writing or content loses its primacy, and may even be overruled. Meanwhile, the internet's authors are no longer simply broadcasting. They're forced to engage in a discussion, whether they like it or not.

Journalism is understandably threatened by this (just as folio scribes were by the printing press in its day) because, for a long time, journalists and editors had dominion over a certain type of information and how it was distributed. As part of my job I edit a newspaper letters page, which is a kind of stone-age social media forum, but, even as it gives the impression of being an honest representation of readers' views, it is still selected and edited by someone with certain views and biases (hard as I try to minimise them). Newspapers and magazines have long tried to show they listen to readers and take their views into account, but there is still a distinct power dynamic at play. If a reader's view isn't welcome, it won't see the light of day on paper. These days, you can delete comments on your newspaper website, granted, but someone can go on Twitter or Facebook or a blog and say whatever they want about you and your work. Unless that person has broken the law by, for example, threatening or inciting violence, there is no way you as an author can stop that from happening. Sometimes, social media criticism of a piece of journalism becomes more widely read and shared than the story itself. We've all read news stories that show this happening, headlined something like 'People on Twitter are angry about this piece arguing millennials are lazy'.

The three main ways publications have responded to this shift in the nature of audience tell you a lot about whether they view it as a threat or an opportunity.

The first and most basic way you might exist on social media as a journalist or a media organisation is to simply post links and content. This is sticking broadly to the Gutenberg model of broadcasting to a large number of people without directly engaging with them, and expecting them to passively consume what you say.

The second method is to approach social media as a source, a kind of water cooler where you pick up information, stories or case studies. Increasingly, journalists are trained to use social media in this way: in a recent study, one in four online stories sampled from around the world contained embedded social media posts.[26]

There's a negative side to this method, though. As a society, we talk about social media as a revolutionary, democratising force, but you don't have to spend very long looking at it to realise this isn't always true. Social media users are, by definition, those with internet access and time to spare (both of which have class implications), and there are a high number of journalists and a relatively small number of what we would call 'normal people' using public social media accounts. Twitter has far fewer users than Facebook, and around two thirds of these are inactive, yet Twitter is often used as a news source simply because most posts are shared publicly. If you post a tweet or public Facebook post about a news event – a photo from a fire, or a video from a terrorist attack – you'll probably be inundated with requests from journalists who desperately want to use it.

Especially in the early days of social media, there was the feeling that material from what are sometimes termed 'citizen journalists' on social networks was very pure and authentic. During the Arab Spring, the media used vast amounts of on-the-ground material, some of which was later shown to be falsified or lacking important context. Gradually, journalists clocked that this was just a source of information like any other and, as such, it required fact-checking and verification. The mental elision by those journalists tells us something about our societal understanding of social media: we assume it is an accurate window onto other people's lives, when, of course, it's as open to falsification or errors as anything else.

Social media also wants us to believe it is democratic and offers a total, rather than partial, upending of the Gutenberg model of broadcasting information. Yet, on many of these social networks (especially the mostly public ones like Twitter), there exists a kind of pyramid structure in which not many people are doing the talking, while millions are doing the listening. The fundamental sadness of Twitter is that it promises to be a leveller: you have a Twitter account, Barack Obama has a Twitter account, Beyoncé has a Twitter account. You can access these faraway figures at the touch of a button. The catch, of course, is that Barack Obama is never going to reply. Beyoncé probably has no particular desire to read your tweets. While social media is hugely disrupting the concept of audience, this is still a gradual process, and it would be a mistake to imagine that these sites are utopias where anyone can speak, and anyone can be listened to.

There is a third way to engage with social media as a journalist or a media organisation. This approach still suffers from the limitations mentioned above, because social media will never be a neutral tool free of social pressures and prejudices. But the most forward-looking way to use these platforms is as a place to have a two-way conversation. Readers can comment on stories, and publications and journalists can reply, or use the information shared to update the story, or pursue a new angle. When publications run live blogs, they come closer to admitting their role in the wider conversation online, by pulling in different sources and demonstrating that knowledge now develops by the minute, not with the publication of 600-word news reports once a day.

When the *Guardian* and other publications around the world reported on the Panama Papers (leaked documents showing offshore tax avoidance), they simply published them online in full so that anyone could read them or uncover stories within them. This is a radical undermining of old journalism's view of power, platform and audience. Journalists are much more used to concepts like embargoes (where information is circulated to journalists in advance but may not be released by them until a specified time) or exclusives (where a publication has a story that no one else has, so can take its time in releasing it). But instead of hanging onto those documents until they could be combed for all possible stories, these newspapers simply threw open the gates, and opened up the information to everyone.

When talking about publications and their audience, an interesting test case is the approach to the comments sections which sit below online articles. At first glance, it would seem clear that fully open commenting gives the audience its chance to talk back, and is a positive development. But online news sites are increasingly shutting their comments sections down, or only opening them on certain articles.

The main reason for this arises from the legal system. Under UK media law, hosting comments on your site is a form of publishing. This means that if someone posts death threats or defamatory claims, and you don't act swiftly to remove them, you could be vulnerable to legal action, just as you would be if you published defamatory comments in your newspaper.

As advertising spending is slashed, and more people consume news online for free, many publications don't have the resources to constantly moderate comments. Meanwhile, there is compelling evidence that comments do not generate nearly enough clicks to be cost-effective.[27]

Wherever you stand on it, this issue shines a useful light on the limits of viewing modern publishing as an online free-for-all. Who moderates it? Who keeps it safe? And who pays for it? We don't know the answers to these questions yet, and it's up to politicians to work with social media companies to make clear where the responsibility lies for, say, monitoring terrorist content or keeping paedophiles from grooming children on social networks.

There is also an argument that online comments on news sites simply aren't conducive to good discussion. In a piece announcing that the left-wing magazine the *New Statesman* would no longer host comments under articles, Helen Lewis, its deputy editor, wrote:

> The idea that disabling comments is returning to a model where journalists told the audience things, and the audience mutely accepted what was slopped out, is nonsense. Even the most generous estimates reckon only 1 per cent of readers leave a comment. So banning them doesn't stop people having their say: it stops one in a hundred people creating an aura of authentic grassroots reaction.[28]

As Lewis understands it, comments sections have become places where only the dedicated critics lurk, and the rest of us simply read, as we read the piece. Later in her article, Lewis suggests that engaging with journalists on Twitter, or even by email, is a better model.

In effect, she argues that there should still be hierarchies of information online. This seems fair. Most commenters are not putting out the same kind or quality of information as someone who has investigated a topic for a year, and has specific training on how to present the information to an audience.

For me, though, the bigger issue is that the discussion in comments sections is heated and often toxic, even more so than on social media. Part of this is accountability. Comments sections often require only a username, which doesn't necessarily identify you, while on social media your posts are linked to a cohesive online identity (though of course, as we see with trolls, that doesn't stop everyone).

Social media has less of the feel of a 'bathroom wall' covered in angry scribbles than the comments section under an article. This is not least because in the act of commenting, or sharing, you publish pieces of content on your own mini-platform, adding your mark as you do so. Comments sections tend to be negative, yet many people on Twitter and Facebook share a lot of things they think their friends would like or enjoy as well as links to things they hate.

By admitting that Web 2.0 has resulted in a giant global conversation, we accept that the role of journalism has radically changed. But this doesn't have to be a negation of its role. The niche role that journalism should now strive to fill is not that of the controller of information, but of its arbiter, verifier and curator. The concept of verified or trusted sources is making a comeback after the outcry over so-called fake news. Social networks themselves now have more emphasis on verified accounts and spam or abuse filters. Google's algorithms, which have a huge impact on the revenue streams of online news sites, deprioritise pages that are poorly written, lack important facts or are plagiarised from elsewhere.

The full consequences of fake news stories (the term originally referred very specifically to purposefully false stories run on the websites of ersatz news organisations) in elections in the US and UK are yet to be fully explored, and there's a chance the impact of this specific phenomenon has been overblown. However, the way the phrase suddenly became central to the discourse around news, and is now used to refer to any story thought to be inaccurate, shows a wider cultural concern around truth. Readers want to be assured that what they're reading is correct, and this is an opportunity for legitimate publications to re-establish themselves as trusted sources.

Despite complete changes in how we use technology, the ways we collect, verify and present information as journalists haven't hugely changed. The kinds of stories people want to read haven't either: we want to know what our politicians are doing, to understand what will keep us and our families healthy, and to laugh and inform ourselves about what it is to be human. The difference now is that journalists have far less of the innate privilege they enjoyed 50 years ago. For those who feel threatened by the rise of social media and online journalism in general, I think it's important to question whether your unease is really about the technology, or whether you feel threatened by the changing power dynamic between journalists and their audience.

In 2006, the year that Facebook and Twitter both went global, the media critic Jay Rosen wrote a piece called 'The People Formerly Known as the Audience'.[29] It is written as an answer to those in the media who, with the rise of blogging platforms (and, soon after, social media sites), have asked, 'If all would speak, who shall be left to listen?' Rosen argues that, like the monks panicked by Gutenberg's invention, these bristling journalists have been witnessing not a threat, but a democratic revolution. Speaking on behalf of readers, he writes, 'Once they were your printing presses; now that humble device, the blog, has given the press to us. That's why blogs have been called little First Amendment machines. They extend freedom of the press to more actors.'

How we all respond to this new balance of power will determine the future of journalism.

The Power of Journalism:
Back to the Future of News

Charlie Beckett

The last ten years have seen a paradox of power for journalists. Overall, the ability of the mainstream news media to set agendas and control information has been drastically diminished. However, individual journalists or acts of journalism can have more impact than ever before. This matters to the journalists, but also to the public, because knowledge is power, and the question of who controls the production and distribution of topical information is more important than it has ever been.

Over the last decade since I left the newsroom and went to run a think tank at the LSE, I have been excited by the increased productive power that new technologies give journalists. Back then, I was especially impressed by the extraordinary potential of digital devices and online networks to make journalism more efficient, engaging and creative. My smartphone had more computing and communicative power than the entirety of some of the broadcast newsrooms I had worked in before.

I also realised that the emergence of new producers, such as bloggers, and new structures, especially social media, would transform the news media. The very ideas of journalism and news would change profoundly. It would create more sources and outlets for mainstream journalists. It would also increase competition and reduce the power of the news media to act as gatekeepers to information. This came at the same time as a financial crisis for journalism as newspaper sales plummeted and advertising revenue switched to new online platforms such as Facebook and Google. Journalism was simultaneously threatened and empowered. Today, much of the news media still looks familiar, but vast swathes have changed in style or format and, most importantly, the relationship between the journalist, the public and the news itself has been radically rearranged.

I was optimistic about the emerging changes. My first book was called *SuperMedia* because I could see how the new technology, working with the reader or viewer, was creating wonderful, novel formats and fresh ways of reaching consumers on different platforms and around the world.[30] I argued that increased public power, such as reader comments or 'accidental' reporting via camera phones, would reduce the dominance of professional journalists. Meanwhile, those journalists who connected to these new networks with enthusiasm and ingenuity would be able to reinvent their product for an age of sharing, interactivity and innovation. Over the last ten years we have seen the evolution of a whole range of new powerful storytelling techniques such as online video, data journalism, multimedia narratives and virtual reality. Journalists have turned to Instagram, Snapchat and Pinterest as well as using search tools and social networks like Facebook to find new audiences and to connect their products to people who want to know. In a complex world full of change and uncertainty, the public appetite for news has grown.

At the same time, the news media has lost much of its control over the distribution of its work. In the past, we made packages of newsprint or broadcast programmes. These were delivered or consumed in a one-way process, usually passively. Now, journalism is increasingly shared according to what the public 'like' online. So emotion has become an important driver of the information economy in all sorts of ways. By 'emotion' I mean literally 'happy', 'sad', 'like', 'don't like'. But more generally, this is about how on networks we respond to information in a personal way. For example, we respond according to our identity or values. We say, 'I am the sort of person who cares about those teenagers protesting about gun laws in America, so I'm going to share news about it.' A lot of the content that you choose to forward or consume doesn't have a utilitarian value. It rarely affects your material life directly. Weather news, for example, might help you decide whether to take an umbrella when you leave the house, but most news is about that emotional response: it makes you feel sad or excited; angry or intrigued; informed, stimulated or simply happy that you have joined in the news ritual. With social media especially, you tend to share news with like-minded communities or as part of networks where other people might respond in similar or conflicting ways. So if journalists want to be powerful, they need to get emotional.

The online explosion of fake news, or misinformation, represents another challenge for journalism, partly related to this more emotion-driven communication. There are different kinds of misinformation, ranging from commercially driven clickbait right through to deliberate lies that seek to discredit certain causes. The range includes relatively harmless false news such as satire as well as intentionally disruptive propaganda that aims to spread confusion and cynicism. It exploits the same viral and social power of online networks that allows good journalism or democratic campaigns to flourish. Sometimes fake news is the product of shadowy organisations, governments or political parties trying to target voters or stir up division and anger, especially around key moments such as elections, events or hot topics. Again, the power is being shifted from the traditional arbiters of what is true and what is important, such as mainstream news organisations. Yet the fake news crisis is good news for credible journalists. The more reliable and accountable news brands have seen a sharp rise in people consuming their content and even paying for subscriptions. When there is such an abundance of questionable material out there, people often turn to more trustworthy sources.

The principal challenge for mainstream news is to not

simply get back its power, but also become more valued. More fact-checking will help. Getting platforms such as Facebook or YouTube to clean up their networks by removing false material or by promoting credible content would be useful. But the long-term solution is not just to police social media. Mainstream media has to stop complaining about its loss of power and start building better connections with the public. To do that, it has to understand why people have turned to those partisan and propagandic sources. It has to become much more diverse and relevant. That means hiring people who reflect the variety of the communities it covers. It means broadening its news agenda to the concerns of the whole range of the public, not just media and political elites. It means joining in the conversations where they are happening, not only expecting the public to come to their paywalled or subscription-based sites. A lot of the reconnecting can happen via digital networks, but it also means getting away from the screen and into the real world.

Journalists have a moral opportunity here. It is also a business opportunity. One option is for journalists to produce clickbait, to pander to the worst impulses of those people attracted by fake news. But there is also an opportunity for journalists to be better curators, filters, or guides in that dark forest of overabundance. Journalists can be much better at identifying what is credible, verifying what is believable and helping citizens get the evidence that they need. Journalists must still do quite traditional things: be critical, bust myths, give context, be accurate. Their job is also to say challenging things and take on those in power or positions of authority. However, they should also have a sense that they are contributing to 'the good life' and to a 'good' society. This is not some woolly ideal. It is a practical service that says journalism can help people to live healthier, happier, more enabled lives as individuals and in communities. Good information is good for us, and journalism can help provide this. This is about journalists empowering the public, not themselves.

Yes, this means more facts, more reporting from the field and more digging through data. But it also means that journalists have to respond at a more 'emotional' level. They have to listen more and adopt the language of their users. They must discover a new sense of human interest. They must be more transparent about their own work. Journalists should always seek to be authoritative and expert. They should find evidence. But the problem of trust at the moment is not an absence of facts. In the end, politics, for example, isn't just about facts; it's about moral choices, values and feelings. So journalism is going to have to learn empathy. To get people's attention, journalists first have to understand people better and be more honest about their own biases. There is nothing wrong with partisan or subjective journalism as long as it is self-critical and clear about where it is coming from.

The good news is that many of the new technologies allow

us to do this. We have more data about how people use and relate to news. We have algorithms that can be designed to promote personalisation, giving people what interests them, but also to offer a richer diet that includes surprises and difference. A combination of artificial intelligence and human judgement and creativity can help people through the maze of information. Instead of the journalist controlling the process, it can become a shared experience of curation and interaction, not delivering a product, but offering a service – and always with the human at the centre of the process.

So, in a way, we are back at the beginning of my decade of 'the future of news'. Yes, we have lost a lot of journalism jobs and even some media organisations, especially at the local news level. However, we have a whole new breed of digital journalists with job titles that didn't exist a couple of years ago. We have new digital native news organisations, from *BuzzFeed News* to *The Bristol Cable*. Mainstream media has been remarkably resilient, retooling newsrooms, discovering new distribution channels and creating new business models including free newspapers as well as membership- and subscription-based ones. About ten years ago, I predicted that we would lose roughly 70% of journalism jobs. That was mainly based on assessing the proportion of journalism that simply duplicates content created by other people, or that could be automated. But although a lot of old jobs went, new ones have been created. Some of these are based outside news organisations in, for example, universities or public relations departments. Others are with third-party agencies that provide specialist journalism services such as aggregation, data visualisation or engagement. Some of the best journalists have become more niche. Almost all the news organisations tell me they're covering fewer topics, but they are trying to go deeper and add distinct value.

There is still the danger of an information gap. People like me, who care a lot about politics and current affairs and who can afford it, are now super-served with high quality accessible journalism. But is the wider population getting enough news that it can use? And is our news media creating the kind of robust but civil debate that makes for healthy communities and national deliberation? The fear of filter bubbles and echo chambers is overblown. We have always had our own world views and we tend to group together. Old media was much more segregated than digital. There is some evidence that social media fosters more diverse news consumption. But even so, we should always want media that connects us and allows argument across identity lines. There is some evidence that a minority of people are avoiding news entirely because they find it too negative, overwhelming and confusing. Journalism should always want their attention, too.

I am back to where I began this decade of journalistic and political upheaval. New technologies, and especially the power of the platforms, threaten journalism. Artificial intelligence and even blockchain could reshape our information infrastructure in more profound ways. But these continuing changes have the potential to empower journalism, if only it can adapt and keep public value at its core. At the moment, the debate is centred around the role of platforms such as Facebook, Google and Twitter and how much more power they have over the flows of news, even though they barely create any journalism themselves. It is an argument that is at the heart of the LSE Truth, Trust and Technology Commission that I am leading at the moment. Clearly, as a society we need to make sure that the information infrastructure that has evolved delivers the kind of news that we want, rather than simply adding profits to the Silicon Valley behemoths. Good journalism needs to be sustained, not drained by the social networks.

Yet perhaps the greatest threat to free journalism is not technology or even market forces. It is an old enemy: authoritarian leaders or governments who see independent journalism as a threat to their power. Around the world there has been a significant increase in the repression of free news media. The tactics are diverse. Some are old-fashioned, such as police or military violence. Journalists are beaten and thrown into jail. Awkward newsrooms are closed down with impunity. But most worrying is that authoritarian politicians and governments are using the same new technologies that can empower journalists to monitor and suppress the news media. Governments are crying 'fake news' at critical reporting. They are using bots to spread disinformation and online trolls to attack dissent and fair comment. The platforms such as Facebook that provide spaces for free expression and protest are struggling to defend open journalism when their networks come under these assaults. This makes it even more important for the news media to rediscover its public role and its social value. It has to reconnect with members of the wider public and convince them of its vital role.

Good journalism has always been under threat. At times it has appeared powerful, even over-mighty. Now it must turn the paradox of power into a recipe for survival. By humbly accepting that it must work with and for the people, perhaps it can save itself.

Notes

1   Ann Leslie, *Press Freedom; Press Responsibility*, dialogue with Nick Robinson and Frances D'Souza, Westminster Abbey Institute, 17th October 2016.

2   Tom Stoppard, *Night and Day* (New York, Grove Press, 1979).

3   Marilynne Robinson, *Integrity and the Modern Intellectual Tradition*, lecture, Westminster Abbey Institute, 7th March 2017.

4   *BBC Annual Report and Accounts 2017/18* (London, BBC, 2018), p. 60.

5   Will Brett, *It's Good to Talk: Doing referendums differently after the EU vote* (London, Electoral Reform Society, 2016), p. 16.

6   Rt Hon Lord Justice Leveson, *An Inquiry into the Culture, Practices and Ethics of the Press* (London, The Stationery Office, 2012).

7   Soroush Vosoughi, Deb Roy and Sinan Aral, 'The spread of true and false news online', *Science*, 9th March 2018, vol. 359, no. 6380, pp. 1146–1151.

8   Claire Foster-Gilbert (ed.), *The Moral Heart of Public Service* (London, JKP, 2017), p. 61.

9   Helen Boaden, 'In Search of Unbiased Reporting in Light of Brexit, Trump and Other Reporting Challenges in the UK and US', *Harvard Kennedy School Shorenstein Center*, 13th June 2017, https://shorensteincenter.org/unbiased-reporting-brexit-trump-uk-us, accessed 8th October 2018.

10   Jean Seaton, *How Impartial?*, dialogue with Gary Gibbon and David Neuberger, Westminster Abbey Institute, 1st November 2016.

11   Nick Robinson, *Live From Downing Street: The Inside Story of Politics, Power and the Media* (London, Bantam Press, 2012).

12   Nick Robinson, *Election Notebook: The Inside Story of the Battle over Britain's Future and My Personal Battle to Report It* (London, Bantam Press, 2015).

13   Gary Gibbon, *Breaking Point: The UK Referendum on the EU and its Aftermath* (London, Haus Publishing, 2016).

14   Charlie Beckett, *SuperMedia: Saving Journalism So It Can Save the World* (Oxford, Wiley-Blackwell, 2008).

15   Charlie Beckett, *WikiLeaks: News in the Networked Era* (Cambridge, Polity, 2012).

16   Robinson, *Live From Downing Street*.

17   Ofcom, *News Consumption in the UK: 2016* (London, Ofcom, 2017).

18 Ofcom, *Attitudes towards the impartiality of television news* (London, Ofcom, 2014).

19 Nick Timothy, 'I've already voted Leave – but these wretched campaigns show everything that's wrong with British politics', *ConservativeHome*, 14th June 2016, https://www.conservativehome.com/thecolumnists/2016/06/nick-timothy-ive-already-voted-leave-but-i-cant-wait-to-get-away-from-this-bloody-referendum-campaign.html, accessed 8th October 2018.

20 Carl Emmerson, Paul Johnson, Ian Mitchell and David Phillips, *Brexit and the UK's Public Finances* (London, Institute for Fiscal Studies, 2016).

21 Simon Kuper, 'Trump, Brexit and the age of broken promises', *Financial Times*, 26th January 2017.

22 Bill Bishop, *The Big Sort: Why the Clustering of Like-Minded America is Tearing Us Apart* (Boston, Houghton Mifflin, 2008).

23 Jonathan Capeheart, 'Why the Knight Foundation president thinks we're living through the biggest disruption since Gutenberg and the printing press', *Washington Post*, 18th October 2016.

24 Ibid.

25 Max Roser, 'Books', *Our World In Data*, 2017.

26 'A SAM Study on Social Embed Usage Across 1,000,000 News Articles', *SAM*, 19th October 2016,

https://www.samdesk.io/stateofembeds, accessed 8th
October 2018.

27   Joel Johnson, 'Comments are Bad Business for Online
Media', *Animal*, 10th April 2012, http://animalnewyork.
com/2012/comments-are-bad-business-for-online-
media, accessed 8th October 2018.

28   Helen Lewis, 'Don't leave a comment: What's the point
of turning the net into a giant lavatory wall?' *New
Statesman*, 12th April 2012, https://www.newstatesman.
com/blogs/internet/2012/04/dont-leave-comment,
accessed 8th October 2018.

29   Jay Rosen, 'The People Formerly Known as the
Audience', *PressThink*, 27th June 2006, http://archive.
pressthink.org/2006/06/27/ppl_frmr.html, accessed
8th October 2018.

30   Beckett, *SuperMedia*.

ALSO IN THIS SERIES

*The Kingdom to Come: Thoughts on the Union
Before and After the Scottish Referendum*
by Peter Hennessy

Commons and Lords: A Short Anthropology of Parliament
by Emma Crewe

*The European Identity:
Historical and Cultural Realities We Cannot Deny*
by Stephen Green

Breaking Point: The UK Referendum on the EU and its Aftermath
by Gary Gibbon

Brexit and the British: Who Are We Now?
by Stephen Green

These Islands: A Letter to Britain
by Ali M. Ansari

Lion and Lamb: A Portrait of British Moral Duality
By Mihir Bose

*The Power of Politicians
(published with Westminster Abbey Institute)*
by Tessa Jowell and Frances D'Souza

*The Power of Civil Servants
(published with Westminster Abbey Institute)*
by David Normington and Peter Hennessy

The Power of Judges (published with Westminster Abbey Institute)
by David Neuberger and Peter Riddell

Drawing the Line: The Irish Border in British Politics
by Ivan Gibbons

Westminster Abbey Institute

The Power of Journalists is published in partnership with Westminster Abbey Institute. Westminster Abbey Institute was established in 2013 to nurture and revitalise moral and spiritual values in public life, inspire the vocation to public service in those working in Westminster and Whitehall, identify and defend what is morally healthy in their institutions and promote wider understanding of public service. The Institute draws on Westminster Abbey's resources of spirituality and scholarship, rooted in its Christian tradition and long history as a place of quiet reflection on Parliament Square.

ALSO IN THIS SERIES

The Power of Civil Servants
The Power of Judges
The Power of Politicians